-7.

29.

-7.

Artificial Climbing Walls

Artificial Climbing Walls

Kim Meldrum and Brian Royle

PELHAM BOOKS

First published in Great Britain by
PELHAM BOOKS LTD
52 Bedford Square
London, W.C.1
1970

07207 0430 8

*Set and printed in Great Britain by
Tonbridge Printers Ltd,
Peach Hall Works, Tonbridge, Kent
in Plantin ten on twelve point
on paper supplied by P. F. Bingham Ltd,
and bound by James Burn at Esher, Surrey*

Contents

Illustrations

Foreword

by H. D. Greenwood
(Hon. Secretary, British Mountaineering Council)

In the past few years, the interest in mountaineering and rock climbing in this country has grown rapidly. An aspect of this growth which is peculiar to the United Kingdom is the development by local education authorities and other bodies of Centres for outdoor pursuits. Starting with the Outward Bound Trust, there are now over 50 such Centres, at many of which mountaineering is a principal subject.

The technique of rock climbing can, however, be taught not only in the hills themselves, but also on artificial rock faces erected for example in gymnasia. In this way, the often limited opportunities for learning climbing techniques in the mountains and rock outcrops themselves can be supplemented by training on artificial rock walls, which can be built anywhere.

The advantages of such facilities are becoming widely realised and appreciated, and the B.M.C. has over the past couple of years received many requests from education authorities and elsewhere, for advice on the design and erection of climbing walls.

It was therefore decided that we should make an investigation of the various designs which were in existence, and collect these, with appropriate comment, into a single publication. Mr Kim Meldrum, the Warden of the White Hall Outdoor Pursuits Centre (Derbyshire Education Committee) and a member of our Committee of Management, kindly offered to undertake the work, and the C.C.P.R. kindly agreed that Mr Brian Royle of their North-West Region, who had already done work on the subject, should collaborate with him. The British Mountaineering Council is indebted to the authors for their detailed investigation of the subject and for their work in the production of this book.

A number of designs of climbing walls are given in the book, but perhaps the most important contribution of the authors is how climbing walls should be designed to incorporate examples of the basic techniques of rock climbing; and how these walls should be used to best advantage.

It is hoped that this book will be useful to all those concerned with the teaching of rock climbing.

The Roaches, a typical
gritstone outcrop about
eighty feet high.
W. A. Poucher, FRPS

2. The Glenmore Polylith; Climbing and
abseiling. Note the use of crash helmets.
E. D. G. Langmuir

3. St Peter's School, Seaford. The simulated Matterhorn. *Fox Photographs Ltd.*

Introduction

Climbing walls embrace not only the indoor and outdoor apparatus which is designed to simulate climbing on natural rock faces, but also includes the use of existing buildings which may or may not have been specifically modified.

The Central Council of Physical Recreation (C.C.P.R.) have been aware of a 'growing evidence of a demand for the inclusion of facilities for training in rock climbing within a sports hall.'[1] One indication of this demand is seen in the increasing number of requests received by the British Mountaineering Council (B.M.C.) for advice and information on climbing walls. As the recognised national body for the sport of mountaineering, the B.M.C. has commissioned this book but, fully realising the necessity for close co-operation with other interested bodies, has been in constant touch with the Central Council.

The purpose of this book is, therefore, to provide information on a wide variety of climbing walls which have been developed in Britain. It is hoped that this work will enable all those who are concerned in the construction, financing and use of climbing walls to make the best possible choice for their own purposes based on the experience of others.

The book does not attempt to provide a definitive list of all the climbing walls in use but it does draw attention to the principle types in use and points out the relative merits and drawbacks of each main type. The selection of type examples is made to illustrate either a special or novel feature or for historical reasons.

It is assumed that the reader will generally not be familiar with the normal technical vocabulary of mountaineering[2] and the more

[1]*Planning For Sport*, p. 56 (C.C.P.R. 1968).
[2]A comprehensive glossary of terms is provided in the '*Encyclopaedic Dictionary of Mountaineering*', P. Crew, Constable 1968.

specialised mountaineering terms are therefore defined in foot-notes.

It is appreciated that many of those responsible for the construction and design of climbing walls may not be familiar with the problems and techniques of rock climbing and, although many books have been written on the subject, it will clearly be of help to underline the essentials of the sport, so that the use of climbing walls can be placed in a realistic context.

It is also necessary to relate the design of a climbing wall to the infinite variety of rock structure. If it is wished to create a man-made microcosm of all the major rock formations, it is necessary to be familiar with the natural rock faces which provide limitless opportunities for developing climbing skill and offer inexhaustible potential for individual rock climbs. At first glance, a cliff face appears to be a vast expanse of bare rock, sheer and unclimbable. A closer look will show that it is often less steep than first impressions indicate and the whole crag will be weathered into buttresses divided by deep vertical gullies. A further examination will reveal ledges often large enough to accommodate several climbers. These ledges or stances are utilised by climbers to divide the steep sections of rock into stages or pitches. Each pitch will vary in length and in the combination of rock formations it contains and may include: walls, slabs, grooves, chimneys, cracks, ribs and overhangs. What was apparently featureless rock reveals itself to be a complexity of formations (Plate 1).

The shape and texture of rock varies from one geological structure to another. The hard rocks of the major mountain regions in Britain offer sharp incut holds and textures varying from the smooth fine grained volcanic tuffs of the Crafnant Valley in Snowdonia to the rough abrasive gabbro of the Cuillin of Skye. Each rock type offers a different texture and characteristic formations. The mountain limestone of the Peak District is steep and riven with many fissures and small incut holds. Not infrequently it throws out a formidable challenge to the climber by presenting huge overhanging walls. The texture and character of limestone contrasts strongly with the coarse grained and rounded holds of the millstone grit which outcrops in the same area and which draws thousands of climbers to the Peak District every week-end.

Yet another rock which provides sport for the climber in the Midlands is the Dolomite limestone found at Brassington, Pleasley and Cresswell. This rock is pitted with a multitude of tiny pocket holds similar in shape and profusion to the formations found in the sandstone outcrops of Kent.

In designing an artificial climbing wall, it is essential to understand the major problems and features found on a rock face and be cognisant with the skills which have to be developed in order to overcome these problems. These may be considered under the following headings:

GULLIES

Gullies are the largest of the vertical rifts which fracture the rock face.

CHIMNEYS

Smaller than the gullies are the chimneys which are vertical clefts wide enough to get into and can be climbed by a variety of methods.

(a) *Backing Up*

Where a chimney is between 2′ and 3½′ wide, it is possible for the climber to place his back against one wall and his feet or knees on the opposite wall. By applying pressure in opposition it is a simple matter to remain lodged in the chimney with very little physical effort. (Fig. I.) In order to progress up or down the trunk can be eased in either direction by momentarily taking the weight on the hands. Once the trunk has been moved, the feet are adjusted to a comfortable position. Sometimes it is possible to assist an upward thrust by pressing downwards with one foot against the back wall (Fig. 2) beneath the climber.

(b) *Wriggling*

In very narrow chimneys, which barely admit the climber, the only means of progression is by wriggling or thrutching. By applying pressure to the containing walls with hands, knees, elbows, toes, heels and even backsides it is possible by the expenditure of a vast amount of energy and vocabulary to make progress.

(c) *Bridging or Straddling*

At the opposite end of the scale the very wide chimney offers a problem which cannot be overcome by either of the methods

15

Fig. 1 Backing up with knee and back

Fig. 2 Backing up with foot

described. The technique devised to climb wide chimneys is known as bridging or straddling. The climber faces directly into or out of the chimney and sets one hand and one foot on each wall (Fig. 3) utilising any irregularities on their surfaces as holds. Limbs

Fig. 3   Bridging on a wide chimney

should be moved one at a time in order to maintain three points of contact. However, it is sometimes possible to take all the weight on the hands and move the feet up simultaneously.

Chimneys are a relatively easy feature to create artificially and should extend vertically for a minimum of 8′. Door frames would be an ideal place to practise backing up if only they were a little higher. Narrow corridors give excellent practice in straddling and as well as climbing up and down it is possible to traverse the length of the passage; a useful skill if the floor has been recently polished. Climbers will already have explored the potential of their offices and homes for practice, but architects and climbing wall designers may not have appreciated this potential and the above are given as simple examples of techniques they may wish to try in order to understand the situations and skill environments they are trying to create.

VERTICAL CRACKS

These are fissures which are too narrow to admit the whole of the body. Cracks can be climbed by using individual holds,

17

but two techniques have been developed which have particular relevance to this feature.

(a) *Jamming*

It is often possible to obtain a secure hold in a crack by inserting the hand and then clenching the fist so that the sides of the hand are held firmly against the sides of the crack (Fig. 4).

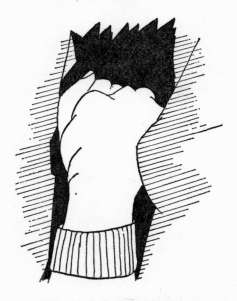

Fig. 4   A fist jam in a crack

In a suitably sized crack approximately 4" wide, this is a secure and relatively effortless hold. Another method of obtaining a firm jam is to slot the hand into a narrow crack (approximately 2¼" wide) and move the thumb across the palm of the hand until the hand is wedged (Fig. 5). It is also possible to obtain a secure foot jam by inserting the foot into a crack and twisting it until it lodges firmly. Other parts of the body can also be used for jamming, i.e. forearms and thighs, depending on the width of the crack, but using hands and feet is by far the most common practice. By using combinations of opposing pressures on the sides of a crack, a variety of jams and sprags can be devised.

18

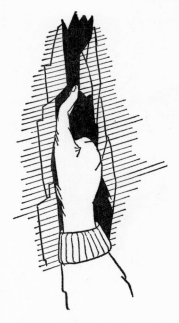

Fig 5 A hand jam in a crack

(b) *Laybacking*

Quite often where the crack is in the corner at the junction of two walls, and sometimes where it is not, it is possible to grip the near edge of the crack and set the feet against the opposite edge or rock face and lift oneself against the pressure exerted by the feet (**Fig. 6**).

Vertical cracks should be $3\frac{1}{2}''$ to $4''$ deep when included in the design of an artificial climbing wall.

HORIZONTAL CRACKS

It is not uncommon to find horizontal cracks or narrow ledges extending across a section of a face and these can be used for finger or toe traverses. Where an artificial climbing wall is constructed in brick, a raked out horizontal joint $\frac{5}{8}''$ wide will provide an adequate finger traverse.

19

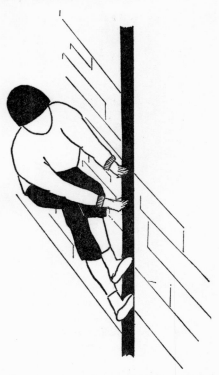

Fig. 6 A layback – a strenuous method of climbing a crack

GROOVES AND CORNERS

These are typical features of most rock faces and are recesses formed where two walls meet; they resemble an open book. They are also known to climbers as diedres. They vary greatly in size, depth and the angle formed by the two walls, some being no more than incipient shallow furrows and yet others may be prominent square cut gashes in the cliff face. It is often possible to climb these features by their individual walls and it is not unusual to find a crack at the junction of the two walls which offers the possibility of jamming or lay-backing. Backing up may also be possible and straddling is often favoured, particularly if the groove overhangs. If this is the case, the body weight can be supported by the legs and the strain taken off the arms by bridging as far out from the junction of the walls as possible, thus keeping the weight over the feet.

RIDGES, ARETES AND RIBS

These are corners turned inside out and they demand no technique specific to the feature although in some cases it is possible to perform a modified layback using holds on the wall for the feet and gripping the edge of the arete with the hands. It may also be possible to grip the rib with the inside of the knees and thighs and 'monkey' up the rock, a technique sometimes described as 'a cheval'.

FACES

These are the stretches of rock between the features already described. Sometimes they are also an integral part of a feature. They are generally defined according to their steepness, measured from the horizontal.

A *glacis* is a very easy angled section of a face where it is often possible to walk unaided by the hands and is nowhere inclined at more than 30°.

Slabs vary in angle between 30° and 60° and often involve delicate climbing on relatively small holds. It is usually possible to keep the weight of the body directly above the feet and is therefore less demanding on the arms than climbing on steeper rock.

Walls are areas of rock set at between 60° and 90°. Good holds are essential as much of the weight is supported by the hands and resting places are at a premium.

Overhangs are sections of rock which tilt beyond the vertical. Extreme overhangs, which may even project horizontally from the rock face, are known as roofs. All overhangs demand strenuous techniques to overcome them and some involve special techniques including the use of artificial aids.

It is unnecessary to create a glacis on the artificial climbing wall as it requires no special skill.

Walls and overhangs are relatively easy to reproduce and the major difficulty is to create a slab (30° to 60°) which is the ideal situation in which to introduce beginners to rock climbing. There are a number of ways in which this can be achieved and these will be discussed later.

INDIVIDUAL HAND AND FOOT HOLDS

All the features that have been described are provided with holds of various shapes and sizes offering many combinations of hand and foot positions. There are limitless permutations of movements and efforts possible, involving pulling and pushing, not only downwards, but also upwards and sideways and sometimes using holds in opposition. The differing shapes and textures of holds have already been discussed earlier in the text. There is, however, one type of hold which frequently recurs in all types

Fig 7 A mantelshelf – a problem frequently met on a rock climb

of rock and should find a place in the design of an artificial climbing wall. This type of hold is known as a mantelshelf and takes its name from the domestic mantelshelf. The climbers' mantelshelf is in fact any horizontal ledge which is backed by a holdless wall or slab. The basic technique is to raise the body by pressing down on the ledge with the hands until the arms are at full stretch, thus allowing one foot to be lifted and placed on the ledge (Fig. 7). The rest of the manoeuvre is completed by pressing down with the foot until a standing position can be attained. The narrowness of the ledge and the steepness of the wall above determine the difficulty of the move. Greater height can be gained in the initial part of the move by pressing up on a clenched fist or on finger tips.

Recommended dimensions for a mantelshelf are included in Chapter II.

ROPE TECHNIQUES

Solitary climbing can be a delight and a challenge to the expert mountaineer. Unroped rock climbing should only be practised when the skills of movement on rock have been completely mastered and when the standard of the climb is well within the capabilities of the climber and the consequences of a slip are fully appreciated.

All beginners and also a very large majority of experienced rock climbers will tackle the sport together with a companion. They do this, not only because of the pleasure that companionship brings with it but also because of the increase in safety that climbing as a member of a team, linked by a rope, can provide.[1]

It is agreed by most mountaineers that the minimum number of climbers ensuring an acceptable level of safety is three. However, two parties of two can climb more quickly on a long route and give a greater feeling of security on remote crags. In designing a climbing wall, it is useful to have a basic knowledge of the techniques involved in safeguarding the members of a climbing team by means of the climbing rope and other items of equipment.

In order to illustrate these principles, the progress of two climbers starting a route is outlined. On arrival at the foot of the crag, they make sure that they are in a safe place, and not likely to be hit by stones dislodged by climbers above. They put on their climbing helmets, take the rope from a rucksack, uncoil it and lay it loosely on the ground. Both climbers tie on to their respective ends of the rope and while the leader, No. 1 surveys the face and studies the line of the route, the second or No. 2 finds an anchor[2] to which he can secure himself.

Anchors are to be found in many shapes and forms. A common one would be a rock spike, another may be a strong tree growing

[1] It is of course possible for a solo climber to devise for himself some measure of protection by the use of the rope and the artificial climbing wall will provide for these skills to be practised.
[2] An anchor is normally referred to as a belay point which is a secure point of attachment for the protection of the climbers.

on a ledge, and yet another may be a chockstone jammed securely into a crack or chimney. If no natural anchor is available, a metal spike or blade, called a piton, is driven into a crack in the rock face. Having found an anchor the second secures himself to it. There are a number of acceptable methods of securing oneself to an anchor. This process is known as belaying. Assuming that the climber has tied the climbing rope directly round his waist, it is then passed round an anchor and brought back through the waist tie, thus forming a loop which is secured by tying round the parts of rope between himself and the anchor and, of course, the waist tie. The climber is now safely tied to the rock face: he is belayed (Fig. 8).

Fig. 8 A belay

No. 2 has belayed himself to a chockstone jammed in a chimney which No. 1 has decided is the best route up the lower section of the cliff. He takes up the rope a few feet from No. 1, allowing him a small amount of slack and passes the rope round his body before taking hold of it. He is wearing gloves because he knows that if No. 1 falls he would be hard put to hold him without protection for his hands and, without this protection, his hands might be severely burnt. No. 1 sets off, first backing up and then wriggling where the chimney narrows. He is heading for a ledge forty feet up. At last he reaches it and finds a small spike of rock to which he can belay himself. Once belayed, he calls down to No. 2 and then hauls in the climbing rope until it is tight between himself and No. 2. He passes the rope round his body, takes a firm hold and brings up No. 2, taking in the rope as No. 2 climbs up to him. When he arrives on the stance, No. 2 attaches himself to the anchor and once he is belayed No. 1 relinquishes his hold on the rope. No. 2 then holds the rope to No. 1 who unties his belay and proceeds up the next pitch. On his way up, No. 1 sees several small spikes and chockstones, and from each he hangs a sling, a small loop of nylon rope, to which is attached a metal snaplink or karabiner. Through this he passes the main climbing rope. This is known as a running belay. The point to notice is that if he does fall off he will only fall twice the distance between himself and the running belay, instead of twice the distance between himself and his No. 2.

In designing a climbing wall, it is essential to ensure that there are sufficient stances and well placed anchors for making belays and running belays.

There are a number of manoeuvres in rock climbing where the rope is of direct assistance to the climber, and the most common of these is abseiling or roping down. Abseiling is a quick, safe way down a rock face when it is not possible or not quick enough to descend by climbing. In order to abseil, the rope is doubled and attached to an anchor. The two ends of the rope are thrown down the face and then the rope is passed round the climber's body (there are several acceptable methods of doing this). The climber then walks backwards down the face leaning well out and holding himself away from the cliff with his feet. By allowing the rope to slide round his body under control, he is able to pick his way down the rock face (Fig. 9). When he reaches the bottom or the next stance, he pulls on one end of the rope to free it from the anchor. A good anchor is obviously essential and a high one, 5' or 6' above the stance, is better than a low one as it facilitates a more comfortable starting position.

It is clearly desirable to place abseil anchors on a climbing wall in a convenient position. However, there may be some merit

Fig. 9   Abseiling

in placing one or two awkwardly in order that practice can be gained in dealing with badly situated anchors. All anchors should be carefully designed and materials used that will easily withstand the heavy loading to which they may be subject.[1] Anchors on external climbing walls should be carefully checked for deterioration due to exposure to the weather and only the best materials, which are available for the production of modern pitons, should be used if metal anchors are favoured. This comment applies to all

[1]This force can be as much as 4000 lbs; the climbing ropes used will have this breaking strain and belay points should also be fully capable of sustaining this load.

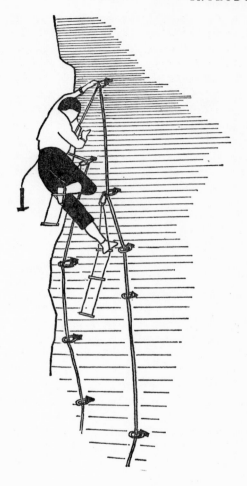

Fig. 10 Artificial climbing techniques

metal anchor points on a climbing wall and not only to those used for abseiling.

The second rope manoeuvre which is increasingly used by experienced climbers is known as artificial climbing, pegging or tension climbing (Fig. 10). The basic technique is quite simple.

27

No. 1 ties onto two ropes; for ease of recognition these are usually of different colours, e.g. red and white. He then hammers a piton into a crack above his head and to this he clips an etrier, which is a short ladder made from loops of nylon webbing or thin nylon rope with metal rungs. The red rope is also clipped to the piton with a snap link. No. 1 then steps into the etrier and the red rope is pulled tight by No. 2 thus holding No. 1 into the piton where he is in a position to reach up and hammer in a second piton. He now repeats the procedure already described using a second etrier and the white rope instead of the red. As he moves up the red rope is relaxed and the white rope takes the strain.

There are many variations on this technique and artificial climbing is becoming increasingly sophisticated.

Although artificial climbing is a technique not normally required by novices, it will nevertheless help to complete the picture of the full range of the climber's armoury of skills.

The organisations concerned in the provision of climbing walls include Local Education Authorities, Private Trusts and Commercial interests; without exception all those who were approached were generous in their assistance; not only did they answer detailed questionnaires but frequently offered architects' plans and photographs of the walls in use. Wherever possible the authors tried to visit the climbing walls selected but they make no apology for basing their observations and recommendations on the comments of those who have been responsible for building them and for using them regularly over a number of years.

The authors are firmly convinced of the value of climbing walls and, although they recognise their limitations, hope that this book will help to stimulate the wise construction of walls in the future and that by so doing the book will add to the pleasures of mountaineers in general and will help to encourage the widespread use of safe climbing techniques.

4. Tonbridge School. An extrinsic wall. *Tonbridge School, Tonbridge, Kent*

5. Stonehill High School, Leicestershire. A small integrated wall. *R. Holmes*

6. Abbotsholme School, Ashbourne. Artificial climbing on an adventitious wall. *David Dean*

7. White Hall Centre, Buxton. The Chapel Traverse. *Daily Mail*

The impulse to climb buildings certainly antedates the sport of rock climbing per se. In Britain, mention has been made of an ascent of King's College Chapel in 1760[1] and 'flying exhibitions' involving the ascent of buildings are recorded from the early part of the eighteenth century.[2]

The end of the 'Golden Era' of mountaineering, defined by Sir Arnold Lunn as ending with the ascent of the Matterhorn in 1865, marked the beginning of rock climbing. In this new branch of the sport, mountaineers sought out routes which did not necessarily lead to the summit and which certainly did not take the easiest line up the cliff. Although climbers were taking an interest in outcrop climbing before the First World War[3] it was not until the period between the Wars that outcrop climbing became a specialised branch of mountaineering almost in its own right. The origin of this degree of specialisation owes much to transport difficulties and to the frustrations which these imposed on the growing numbers of climbers from the industrial regions of the North of England. It is no surprise, therefore, to find that climbers cloistered in Cambridge University should also at this time have sought an outlet for their frustration by climbing on the Colleges.

The Cambridge climbers fell into two categories; those who regarded these expeditions as a substitute for real mountaineering and who therefore used all the normal safety techniques available

---

[1]Whipplesnaith. *The Night Climbers of Cambridge* p. 135 (Chatto and Windus 1937).

[2]E. Byne and G. Sutton *High Peak* p. 27 (Secker and Warburg 1966).

[3]J. Laycock *Some Gritstone Climbs* (Manchester Refuge Printing Dept 1913).

at the time and, on the other hand, those who regarded the sport as a novel and stimulating pastime but having no reference to mountaineering. The first ascent of King's College Chapel by climbers, in the modern sense, was made in the 1920s.

The breakdown of social barriers brought about by two World Wars coupled with increased incomes and leisure time brought about an amazing increase in the popularity of the sport. Between 1945 and 1968 the number of climbers in Britain increased fourfold from about ten thousand to over forty thousand.[1] The significance of this increase has been appreciated by educationalists who have made efforts, in a variety of ways, to direct this rising popularity to educational ends. Impetus was given to this educational policy through the reports of the Wolfenden Committee[2] the Albemarle Committee[3] and the Newsome Committee.[4] It is no surprise therefore to find that the rapid increase in the development of residential training centres and the construction of climbing walls occurred in parallel, both dating from the early 1960s.

The principle of climbing walls cannot truly be said to be a British invention but, because of the educational support that mountaineering has received in Britain, the principle has certainly been developed on a larger scale than anywhere else in the world. The first purpose built wall is thought to have been American; the Schurmann Rock[5] (Fig. 11) in the William G. Long Camp just outside Seattle, which was built in 1941, bears a striking resemblance to the outdoor wall built at the Scottish Council of Physical Recreation's Centre, Glenmore Lodge, in 1968 (Fig. 12: Plate 2). The French were experimenting with adjustable wooden walls in the late 1950s[6] but it was not until

---

[1]K. I. Meldrum *How Many Climbers* Fell and Rock Climbing Club Journal 1968.

[2]*Report of the Wolfenden Committee* (Central Council of Physical Recreation).

[3]*Report of the Albemarle Committee* (H.M.S.O.)

[4]*Report of the Newsom Committee* (H.M.S.O.)

[5]Formerly the Monitor Rock.

[6]Gason Rebuffat demonstrates the use of these walls in '*Rock and Ice*'.

Fig. 11 Schurmann Rock in the William G. Long Camp at Seattle. Built in 1941, it is thought to have been the first of the climbing walls to have been deliberately constructed

1960 that the first wall was built in Britain. It is paradoxical that this wall should have been situated at the Ullswater School at Penrith (Plate 9), in an area where there are many natural rock outcrops. From this first experimental wall the Cumberland Education Authority have continued to develop their early ideas and to introduce more complex schemes. The Wyndham Tower

Fig. 12 The Glenmore Polylith. Built in 1968, it is similar in construction to the Schurmann Rock

31

built in 1965 represents the culmination of these experiments and was at that time the most advanced and certainly the most costly wall in Britain, involving not only a large and complex wall but also a specially constructed tower block to house it. This work has certainly placed the Cumberland Authority among the leading innovators in this field. It is worth noticing that the Cumberland Walls are generally indoor and their existence owes more to the inclemency of the weather than to the lack of natural climbing facilities. The Ullswater wall has proved to be the most widely copied type and has been used in only slightly modified forms on both the interior and exterior of buildings.

Commercial interests were not slow to realise the potential market for climbing walls and considerable thought was given to the problem of portability and adjustability. The first adjustable walls were marketed as early as 1963 and by 1969 there are now four manufacturers offering a variety of walls (Plates 16, 17, 18). Commercial interest also expresses itself in the interest shown by some mountaineering equipment retailers who have started to make climbing walls available to their customers. One of the most recent potential developments is in the interest shown by all sorts of organisations who are enquiring about the best ways in which they can make use of blank walls frequently up to seventy feet high.

The walls have become so adaptable and their value and use is so well established in Britain that in the future most plans for schools, youth clubs and sports halls will incorporate some climbing facilities. There is no doubt that these walls will become more sophisticated and may become larger and more expensive but, in spite of their relatively recent introduction, their evolution has been rapid and the number of significant modifications which are now possible must already be fairly limited.[1] The fact that this pattern of development has been so accelerated and that an established norm has already evolved clearly indicates that there was a serious need for such apparatus.

[1]Edinburgh City have announced plans to construct an interior wall in their Meadow Bank Sports Centre which is to be open for the Commonwealth Games in 1970. The wall will be 72 feet by 45 feet and is estimated to cost £8,000.

8. Drake's Island Adventure Centre, Plymouth. *B. Cilgan, Plymouth Photos Ltd.*

9. Ullswater School, Penrith. The first of the Cumberland walls. *Charles Wilson*

10. Liverpool University. A typical purpose built indoor wall. *Liverpool University*

2 Use and Purpose of Climbing Walls

'Climbing walls should never be regarded as an end in themselves but purely as a means to an end'

In the preceding chapter the growth of mountaineering and rock climbing in particular has been outlined and as the demand for basic training grows so also the highest levels of achievement rise and there is therefore a desire amongst established climbers to improve their performance.

The first requirement for a climbing wall is to provide a training facility on which beginners can learn the elementary skills of movement on a vertical or near vertical plane and also acquire the basic skills of rope handling, *belaying*[1] and *abseiling*.[2] A second purpose is to provide a training medium for the maintenance and improvement of skill, strength and endurance for the more experienced rock climber and for the practice of advanced ancillary techniques, e.g. mountain rescue.

The climbing wall in a school gymnasium appears to have yet another function, apparently of secondary importance, which may appeal strongly to the Physical Educationist. If the apparatus is limited in height, but is varied and offers a challenge at all levels of skill, it can provide a fresh exciting element in the range of physical activities and new challenges can be devised by the enterprising teacher. Rock climbing apparatus providing this element of adventure is being increasingly used by the Physical Education Teacher who has no special interest in introducing rock climbing as an aspect of his programme. It is being recognised by the Physical Education profession as a valuable piece of apparatus for stimulating a rich variety of physical activity.

Let us now examine the basic requirements of a wall which

[1]Belaying: the method of attachment to the rock to safeguard oneself or another member of the group.
[2]Abseil: a method of rapid descent using the frictional property of a double rope wrapped round the body.

has been designed with the needs of a raw beginner in mind. This must provide opportunity for: —

(a) Practice in the basic skills of movement on rock.
(b) Teaching of rope techniques.
(c) Conditioning to the vertical or near vertical environment.

As the artificial ski slope prepares the skier for the elements of movement on snow, so the simulated rock face prepares the rock climber for this first enjoyment of safe movement on a mountain crag or outcrop. The apparatus should therefore include the following: —

(a) Belaying points effectively positioned for teaching and also for securing a leader.
(b) Belaying points for demonstrating *running belays*[1] and for securing climbers practising on the wall.
(c) Belaying points at a high level provided with adequate *stances*[2] large enough to accommodate two climbers in order that pitch[3] climbing can be simulated and abseiling practised. Additional points of attachment set to one side of the stances are necessary for abseiling.
(d) A safety rail or fixed rings at the top of the wall from which *top ropes*[4] can be attached to safeguard users of the wall, whether leading or seconding. A rail along which the ropes can slide has an obvious advantage over fixed points as it enables traverses to be made whilst protected by a rope secured perpendicularly from above the climber and so eliminates any danger of inconsidered pendules.
(e) Rock features, including *slabs,*[5] *walls,*[6] *overhangs,*[7] *aretes,*[8]

[1]Running belay: a dynamic belay used to limit the fall of a leader while actually climbing.
[2]Stance: a ledge where a belay can conveniently be made.
[3]Pitch, the section of a climb between two stances.
[4]Top ropes: A method of using ropes from above for protection.
[5]Slab: An inclined rock plane, generally up to 60° to the horizontal.
[6]Wall: an inclined plane steeper than a slab.
[7]Overhang: a section of a wall which exceeds the vertical.
[8]Arete: a sharp steep ridge of rock.

cracks,[1] *corners,*[2] *grooves,*[3] and *chimneys.*[4] These should be placed in such a position that they offer opportunity for basic techniques to be readily taught and confidently assimilated at a low level. Provision should also be made for these techniques to be practised at a greater height.

The apparatus should be sufficiently high to give a feeling of *exposure*[5] which will in turn motivate a serious attention to the safety techniques and rope handling drills which can be thoroughly practised in a controlled situation.

The pupil's reaction to heights, his speed of learning, physical abilities and aptitudes can be observed and noted by the teacher or instructor and some assessment of his probable reaction and ability in the real situation can be made. If time allows, the pupil's deficiencies and weaknesses can be remedied before he is confronted with the actual mountain situation. By constant attention to detail and thorough training in safety habits and rope handling drills, responsible attitudes are developed and reinforced.

Let us now turn to the provision of facilities for the more experienced climber. His special needs are a training aid providing an opportunity for:—
(a) Maintenance and development of strength and endurance.
(b) Continued conditioning to 'exposure'.
(c) Maintenance and improvement of skill.
(d) Practice in advanced techniques:—
    (i) Tension climbing.
    (ii) Advanced rope techniques, e.g. *prussiking.*[6]
    (iii) Mountain rescue techniques.

[1]Crack: narrow fissure, usually qualified as either wide, shallow, etc.
[2]Corner: angle formed by two planes at right angles.
[3]Groove: a shallow steep V shaped depression running up the rock.
[4]Chimney: a vertical crack which is wide enough to admit a climber.
[5]Exposure: the awareness of height and vulnerability.
[6]Prussiking: a method of climbing a fixed rope using either mechanical devices or frictional knots.

The climbing wall should therefore include the following additional features:—

(1) Simulated climbing situations providing climbing problems at all levels of difficulty and, in particular, climbs of higher grades. If the wall is to provide training in strength, endurance and skill, it should be so constructed as to have inherent inbuilt difficulties offering a fierce challenge to the expert and at the same time motivating those less expert to greater physical effort and improved technical performance.

(2) Provision for practice of advanced and ancillary techniques should include:

(a) Ring bolts set at intervals to simulate *pitons*[1] which are used in *tension climbing*.[2] The basic requirement is for a series of bolts set one above another providing a straight forward succession of attachments in order that the sequence of movements involving the clipping in of ropes, *karabiners*[3] and *etriers*,[4] etc. may be learnt in a simple situation. Further progression in this technique can be affected by clipping into alternate ring bolts, thus giving practice in the use of the top rungs of the etriers. If space allows a whole section of the structure can be devoted to tension climbing providing in addition to a single line route the opportunity for horizontal and diagonal traversing and even the climbing of overhangs.

(b) A platform sufficiently large to accommodate a mountain rescue stretcher and six climbers. The platform must be adequately provided with belay points and should not overhang the wall. This requirement can probably only be met by the structures referred to as Polyliths.

DIMENSIONS OF FEATURES

The dimensions of features such as chimneys, cracks and belay stances are of great importance if the maximum benefit is to be derived from their provision. The table on page 38 sets out the

[1]Pitons: Metal spikes driven into the rock.
[2]Tension climbing: Climbing with direct assistance of the rope.
[3]Karabiner: An oval metal link including a spring loaded gate. Often called a Krab or Snaplink.
[4]Etrier: Short 3-runged rope ladder used in climbing with pitons.

recommended basic dimensions. These will obviously be modified where specific training situations are envisaged. An example of this could be where belay stances and fixtures for running belays are so restricted by size or position to create situations where the climber finds it necessary to manipulate his equipment (ropes, karabiners, slings, etc.) with one hand – a common climbing situation requiring practice.

Where concrete fins and platforms are used in the construction, they should be given a rough cast finish and shuttering should be advantageous to the climber. Smooth finishes should be avoided where possible.

ADAPTABILITY

Some structures will be sufficiently large to allow for the provision of all the above features to be included and, with careful adjustment or *tuning*[1] during the building of the wall, varying standards of difficulty can be built into the wall giving climbing routes of all grades. However, many others will have insufficient surface area to develop individual routes of varied standards and difficulties and it is necessary to devise a method of adjusting the wall to ensure that a variety of problems may be set by the teacher or by the climber himself.

This flexibility has been incorporated into the design of many of the walls at present in use, and they can be readily adjusted to suit the needs of the individual. Modifying or adjusting is achieved by varying the angle of a section of the wall and by the use of movable or adjustable holds which can vary from the semi-permanent holds inserted into sockets or receptacles built into the wall, to holds that are plugged into a frame resembling a large peg board. These holds can be shaped, textured and arranged to resemble the detailed rock features encountered on a climb. There is also the self imposed adjustment which approximates to the climber's game of 'bouldering'. In the real situation climbers frequently set themselves tasks and impose limitations purely for the fun of solving a difficult or technical problem. The direct route on the Eiger is an example of this, and for many years rock climbing routes in Britain have had artificial limitations

[1]Tuning: Adjusted for difficulty.

Feature	Skill to be Practised	Dimensions
Chimney	Back and foot Bridging	2' 6" wide 2' deep or more 4' 0" wide 2' deep or more
Jamming cracks	Fist jam Hand jam Foot jam	3½" wide 4" deep 2/2¼" wide 4" deep 2/3½" wide 4" deep
Belay Stance	Belaying	3' × 18"
Belay Anchor	Belaying	4'/6' above stance
Line of pitons (ring bolts)	Tension climbing	2' 3" intervals when placed vertically one above another.
Mantelshelves	Mantelshelf	8" (minimum) projecting from a vertical wall where no hand holds are available on the wall above the Mantelshelf and the shelf itself is 3' long.
Finger cracks	Various	⅝" – normally raked out joints in the brickwork.
Nutting cracks[1]	Chocking or nutting for running belays or belaying.	1. Sections of jamming cracks narrowed at certain points to facilitate the jamming of artificial chockstones. (Fig. 13).
N.B. The Diagrams show the feature constructed in brickwork. The same feature can be easily devised in other materials.		2. Pre cast nutting blocks. (Fig. 14). 3. Raked out vertical joint in contiguity with a recessed hold. (Fig. 15).
Individual foot and hand holds.	Various.	½" to 4" projected or recessed.

[1]Cracks into which it is possible to jam metal wedges which are themselves attached to loops of nylon or wire and used for running belays or for belaying on stances. The metal wedges are also known as nuts or artificial chockstones and by a variety of trade names.

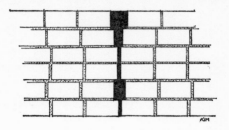

Fig. 13 Irregular jamming cracks, suitable for the insertion of artificial chockstones

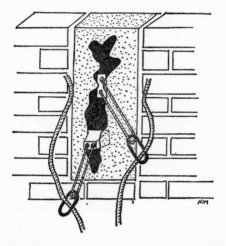

Fig. 14 Precast concrete nutting blocks built into a brick wall

placed on them. In a climber's guide book the Central route on the *Idwal Slabs*[1] is described as follows:—

'This route is very artificial as it follows a rigid non-natural line. The original idea that the use of scratched holds should be eschewed has had to go by default, as almost every possibility has been touched by nails. One can therefore make one's own route.'

[1]The Idwal Slabs is a well known cliff in North Wales.

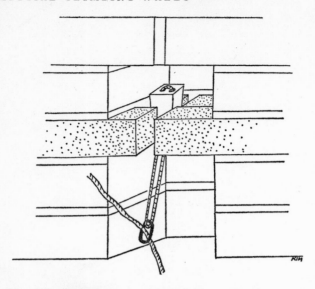

Fig. 15 Raked out vertical joint in brickwork in conjunction with a recessed brick. Note the shaping of the two shaded bricks

On a smaller scale, climbers frequently play the same game on boulders, limiting the number of holds that can be used as hand holds or foot holds, or in some cases, even forbidding touching an eliminated hold by any part of the body – a game of vertical hopscotch. This becomes extremely competitive and holds are eventually reduced to the absolute minimum. This approach has been adapted to the artificial structures and already a number of refinements to the game have been devised.

It is difficult to give an objective evaluation of the contribution made by climbing walls to the general standard of skill and competence displayed by climbers in the real situation. However, the authors are convinced of their value and feel that the enthusiasm for the walls, wherever they are situated is sufficient evidence to give impetus to their further development.

The purpose built climbing wall at Liverpool University provides both training facilities for beginners and experts and is used

11. West Common Sports Centre, Scunthorpe. A versatile and adaptable indoor wall. *R. Holmes*

12. Wyndham School, Egremont. The Wyndham Tower. *Wyndham School*

by an average of 300 climbers per week. These include students under instruction in the Department of Education, climbing club members and groups from other colleges and outside organisations. The Department of Education has found the wall meets the needs of both beginners and experts.

The climbing wall at the West Common Sports Hall at Scunthorpe is a relatively new facility, yet in six months the figures of climbers using the wall has risen to 150 per week and the Youth Service Officer responsible for its development is convinced of its value as a means of introducing the novitiate climber to the basic skills and for providing practice for the more experienced. In the few months that this wall has been in use, there has been a tremendous increase in the achieved standard both on the artificial wall and in the real situation.

Another new development is the intrinsic wall at Tonbridge School, where there is a growing interest in its use both by climbers and others who use it as a stimulating activity. Over 70 boys per week receive rock climbing training or use the wall for enjoyable exercise.

In 1965 the Physical Education Department at Leeds University modified a section of an internal wall by adapting the brickwork and by inserting natural rock holds into the wall. A deliberate attempt was made to design a wall which would interest the experienced climber and routes of high technical standard have been developed. The wall was painstakingly tuned and now provides the stimulus which draws 150 climbers per week to take up its challenge.

The Cumberland Education Authority has been in the forefront in the development of climbing walls in Britain and eleven of its secondary schools now have equipment ranging from the basic wall first built at Ullswater in 1960, which has influenced design throughout the country, to the elaborately constructed Wyndham Tower. One may consider that building a climbing wall in the Lake District is akin to carrying coal to Cockermouth but they do provide a convenient all-weather facility which can also be used at night under artificial lights. Undoubtedly the Cumberland Education Authority has found them to be of great value, and is continuing to experiment and to develop the range of these facilities.

41

The advantages of the artificial wall have been recognised at Glenmore Lodge, the Scottish Council of Physical Recreation's Centre for Outdoor Pursuits in the Cairngorms, where a large Polylith has recently been constructed, and at Plas y Brenin, National Mountain Centre set in the heart of Snowdonia, a small indoor wall has been in use for many years.

Guide books to walls have made their appearance and routes have been recorded by means of colour codes, numbered holds, and by limiting areas of the wall, e.g. high and low girdle traverses. There is little doubt that a hard route will attract local climbers to an artificial wall in the same way that an outstanding climb will draw climbers to a particular crag. Yet another virtue of the climbing wall is that it provides a focal point for climbing activities, drawing together those with an interest in the sport and in winter months, when evening climbing is not practical, it gives an opportunity for both practice and social intercourse.

Necessarily the comments on the use of climbing walls has been general, and the details which give particular walls their individuality and their inherent advantages and disadvantages will be discussed in the following chapter.

3 Exterior Walls

From generalisations on the use and purpose of climbing walls, already considered in the previous chapter, it is apparent that there is an almost bewildering combination of types available and, in order to make a detailed study, it is necessary to develop a coherent system of classification. Although in some ways an unsatisfactory division, the walls have been grouped as either outdoor or indoor; this is unsatisfactory because a number of types can be used equally well in either situation. Within each of these main groupings it has proved convenient to make further subdivisions so that seven quite distinct types are examined. The examination is considered from the point of view of the advantages and the disadvantages of each system which necessarily involves a consideration of the cost of the wall and the cost of maintenance, together with aspects of safety and adaptability. In each section, examples are provided together with locations and photographs illustrating particular wall types or special features. Wherever photographs are unable to show clearly, the methods of construction line diagrams have also been included in the text.

The exterior climbing walls fall into four quite distinct categories, each offering a slightly different range of climbing. These have been arranged in order of exclusiveness and it is no accident that this order should also reflect the cost of construction; those structures which serve no purpose other than climbing are clearly the most expensive.

Based on these considerations, the types to be considered are:—
(1) Polyliths.
(2) Extrinsic Walls.
(3) Integrated Walls.
(4) Adventitious Walls.

1. POLYLITHS

(i) Schurmann Rock, Camp Long, 5200 – 35th S.W. Seattle 6, Washington, U.S.A.

(ii) Glenmore Lodge, Aviemore, Inverness-shire, Scotland.

(iii) St Peter's School, Seaford, Sussex.

For want of any other term, Polylith is used to describe the massive and angular blocks of masonry which have been specially constructed as simulated rock climbing features. As was mentioned in the historical section, the first wall of this type was *Schurmann Rock* at Seattle (Fig. 11). This wall, built of local stone to a maximum height of twenty six feet, offers the best example of this type; on one side there is easy scrambling and on the other side there are difficult routes. The easy aspect does not require the use of ropes whereas the more difficult side offers opportunities for the use of most types of mountaineering equipment and includes chimneys and overhangs. The absence of cracks suitable for jamming is not surprising, since that was a peculiarly British development and one which did not occur until middle 1950s. Climbing instruction is only permitted on the more difficult side if the group is under the instruction of a competent climber and, even then, each climber is expected to have a working knowledge of knots and the principles of belaying. The climbing area of the William G. Long Camp also incorporates an area of irregular stepping stones which is designed to improve balance and movement in rough mountain country. The ultimate in mountaineering simulators is found in the 'concrete glacier' which affords practice in glacier techniques.

The apparent similarity between Schurmann and the *Glenmore* polyliths (Fig. 12, plate 2) is purely accidental. Both were the result of independent thought, and, on closer examination, it will be seen that the similarity is only superficial. The Glenmore wall is a truncated pyramid built on a square base with sides of about thirty feet. The height of the wall is also about thirty feet. Each of the faces offer a variety of routes, but even the easiest of the faces would require the use of ropes for novices. The structure provides examples of all types of holds and rock movements, including opportunities for simple mountain rescue demonstrations and practices. Constructed of massive blocks of local granite by the Royal Engineers, it is difficult to assess the total cost. The cost

13. Leeds University. A simply modified interior brick wall. *Leeds University*

14. A natural rock fragment substituted in the brick wall. Leeds. *Leeds University*

15. Meadow Boys' Club, Nottingham. Practice for climbing overhangs by artificial techniques. *Meadow Boys' Club*

16. Windsor School, Solihull. The Hunt wooden climbing wall. *Hunt & Sons Ltd.*

of the cement alone was about £80; taking labour and cost of transport of the materials into account, a realistic price would be more like £1,500.

St Peter's School

The most recent experiment along these lines has been undertaken at *St Peter's School, Seaford* (Plate 3), where a four faced 32-feet high construction has been modelled as a scaled down replica of the top of the Matterhorn. The base is concrete and the first ten feet are built of masonry, while the upper two thirds are constructed from a tubular steel framework covered with hessian, wire netting, expanded metal and concrete; the hollow mountain so formed is used as a club room. Safety precautions are rigorously observed and no students are permitted to climb higher than 6 feet without using ropes; even below 6 feet they are obliged to have a fielder who is responsible for catching the climber if he falls.

Although the previous three walls attempt to reproduce not only the problems of rock climbing but also the mountaineering atmosphere, recent developments in Germany (Fig. 16) provide the rock climbing aspect with no attempt to simulate the right environment.

Fig. 16 A modern roughcast concrete climbing complex at Munich

All the polyliths are situated outdoors; their massive construction militates against their indoor use. In spite of the obvious disadvantages afforded by inclement weather conditions, these walls copy most faithfully the irregularities of a natural rock outcrop and there is therefore no doubt that, if carefully constructed, they can offer the most realistic climbing. Their principle use lies in the residential mountain centres, where basic instruction in rock climbing is undertaken almost every day and where transport or walking time can be reduced to a minimum.

The cost of this type of wall may prohibit its widespread development and considerable economy can be made by combining its use as a climbing wall with some other purpose.

2. Extrinsic Walls

(i) Tonbridge School, Tonbridge, Kent.

The term 'extrinsic' is used to describe those walls which serve a secondary purpose other than the structural fabric of a traditional building. Only one wall of this type is known to the authors but, in view of the financial saving over the polyliths, it may well become more popular. This wall, situated at *Tonbridge School* (Plate 4) was designed by John Mill, the architect who was responsible for the Liverpool wall and who is himself an enthusiastic climber. It was built in 1968, and its three walls at right angles serve as a climbing wall on the outside and a solid fuel store on the inside. The highest part of the wall is twenty four feet and the total length of the three walls is seventy six feet. Although the boys from the school had prepared the foundations, the total cost of the structure was still £1,519. The actual holds on the outer wall were prepared by leaving some bricks projecting by amounts varying from a quarter of an inch to two inches. A number of spaces were also left which made it possible for members of the London Mountaineering Club to tune the wall in a matter of four hours by inserting additional bricks where necessary to make the climbs possible. This tuning has resulted in the provision of a girdle traverse and fifteen quite independent climbs, some of which are of great technical difficulty. Belay points are provided four feet below the top of the wall on both sides. Because the wall is only constructed of single thickness brick, it would be unsafe to have belay points actually at the top but, in order to protect climbers gaining the top, a rope is used through a sling and karabiner which just reaches the top of the wall from a belay on the opposite side. From reasons of economy and because all the climbing is done on a top rope, polypropylene ropes are used exclusively. The wall has not required any maintenance in spite of considerable use. It is used on five or six afternoons each week as an optional activity and by the school Combined Cadet Force; all of whom spend at least three sessions on the wall. It is occasionally used during normal physical education periods. Climbing clubs from outside the school, together with local Police Cadets are encouraged to make use of the facilities. The success of the wall, certainly among those who use it regularly, can be summarised in the words of one boy who said 'I'd as soon climb here as on Harrison's.'[1]

3. INTEGRATED WALLS

    (i) Lancaster University, Indoor Recreation Centre, Bailrigg, Lancaster. (See book cover.)

    (ii) Stonehill High School, Birstall, Leicestershire. (Plate 7.)

From the general appearance of the Lancaster wall it is no surprise to discover that the design was strongly influenced by the indoor wall at Liverpool University which in turn was inspired by the early Cumberland Walls.

The Lancaster Wall is constructed on the outside west wall of the Recreation Centre and forms the first phase of a more elaborate sports complex which, in time, will enclose the wall so that it will form one wall of a connecting passage between two recreational complexes. It was opened in October 1967, and was planned by Keith Hunt of Tom Mellor and Partners of Lytham St Annes, Bill Slater, the Director of the Liverpool Sports Centre, was consulted as an external adviser. The wall itself measures some fifty feet by fifty feet and, like the Liverpool Wall, the holds are provided by protruding and recessed bricks and by concrete shelves and flanges. This construction allows for most technical movements encountered in natural climbing. The belays

[1]Harrison's are nearby sandstone outcrops which are regularly used by climbers from the South East of England.

47

are provided by metal rings cemented into the brickwork at regular intervals and by a horizontal steel bar running across the top of the wall. The cost of the wall is difficult to establish, since the wall itself forms an integral part of the structure of the sports hall; the additional cost of incorporating the climbing features was about £500 of which the architects fee represents about £65.

The wall is used not only by the University Climbing Club but also by any member of the University or outside organisation who is granted permission to use it. The extent of the use has been difficult to gauge, but a survey conducted during a cold week in February 1968 indicated that three or four people used it every day. The figures for use during the warmer summer months are not known, but it is clear that the wall is never overcrowded. In spite of this it has been found necessary to prohibit the use of nailed footwear and to discourage the use of Vibram soles. By restricting footwear to gym shoes or P.A. type of boots, wear on the holds is reduced to a minimum.

Based on the comments on the principle users, improvements could be made to the wall by reducing both the size and the number of the holds and by extending the wall round a corner of the building and thus introduce a further feature and incorporate elements of anticipation and remoteness. The process of tuning the wall is again seen to be a necessary part of the evolution of a satisfactory wall.

The personal safety of climbers is partly covered by allowing only members of the University Climbing Club to use the wall without express permission. All other users must seek permission on each occasion. To reduce the risk of a serious accident, the use of a top rope is obligatory for everyone but, because the wall is not supervised, this safety factor is very often overlooked. So far there has been only one minor accident but, nevertheless, this has raised the question of insurance. Formerly, all the students at Lancaster were covered by an overall policy taken out by the University, but this scheme has now been dropped and individual students are responsible for their own insurance cover. People from outside the University are allowed to use the wall at their own risk and on the understanding that the University accepts no liability. A notice to this effect is prominently displayed at the foot of the wall.[1] *Stonehill High School, Birstall, Leicestershire* (Plate 5).

The exterior of the end wall of a single storey block of class rooms was modified during construction to give an excellent inexpensive training facility. The wall measures 20 feet by 16 feet and is surmounted by a metal rail which provides a safety rail for those reaching the top of the climbs, and also a continuous belaying point. Built of engineering brick, the wall uses projecting and recessed bricks to provide individual hand and foot holds and concrete platforms provide mantelshelf and overhang problems. A chimney has been created by building parallel vertical brick buttresses.

The wall is unambitious in its aims and yet provides a first-class training ground for the beginner. Boys from the school train on the wall before visiting neighbouring rock outcrops and the lessons learnt and the time saved by first practising on the school's own climbing wall readily justify its construction.

4. ADVENTITIOUS WALLS

 (i) Horspath Bridge and Tunnel, Oxford.
 (ii) Cambridge Colleges.
 (iii) Abbotsholme School, Rochester (Plate 6).
 (iv) Drake's Island, Plymouth (Plate 8).

The introduction made reference to climbing on existing buildings and to the fact that such climbing has existed for many years, indeed long before rock climbing, as a modern sport was seriously entertained. Modern architectural styles and current building methods and materials do not lend themselves to buildings suitable for simulated rock climbing. It is therefore to the architectural heritage of the Industrial Revolution that modern climbers turn in search of practice areas. The massive public works inspired by the extension of the railways in the middle nineteenth century provide excellent opportunities, particularly since they occur throughout the country and are often found in

[1]The notice reads: 'The University of Lancaster shall not be liable for personal injury or damage to property of unauthorised persons caused by or arising out of the climbing of this rockfaced wall and/or ropes attached.'

regions where no natural climbing is available. With the closure of may branch lines, these constructions may become increasingly available.

A well known example of this type is *Horspath Bridge* just outside Oxford. The bridge is constructed from massive blocks of jurassic limestone and small holds between the blocks and within the blocks themselves provide technically difficult climbing requiring considerable finger strength. There are about a dozen routes ranging from difficult to very severe and include walls varying from seventy degrees to vertical. The longest routes traverse through the bridge and are about sixty feet long; the highest routes are about twenty feet. The arch of the bridge gives good practice in artificial climbing. The nearby Horspath Tunnel presents quite a different problem.[1] The Tunnel facing is made of brick and the holds are frequently small drainage pipes which protrude for only a fraction of an inch. The wall itself is about thirty five feet high at its highest point and some one hundred and fifty feet long. The wall is concave, becoming progressively steeper towards the top where a cornice a few feet below the parapet provides a difficult mantelshelf.

Mention has already been made of climbing on the buildings in *Cambridge*. Apart from the very obvious difficulties in obtaining permission for such undertakings, there are, in addition, inherent dangers from the poor state of much of the masonry on any such old buildings. In general, therefore, climbing of this type is rightly deprecated, not only because of the personal danger involved but also because of the danger of damaging the buildings themselves.

A very simple modification of existing walls of little architectural merit can be achieved by the insertion of a few pitons or bolt brackets. This has recently been done at *Abbotsholme School* (Plate 6), where artificial climbing can be taught and perfected. This type of climbing is of very limited appeal and its use as a vehicle for basic rock climbing instruction is even more limited. It does, however, provide those who are already conversant with the basic techniques an opportunity to increase their arm strength

[1]Oxford University Mountaineering Club Journal 1957 p. 26 O.U.M.C.J. 1960 pps. 18–20.

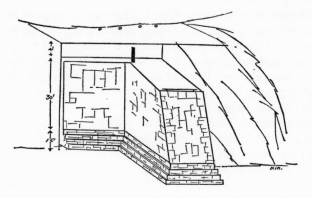

Fig. 17 Drake's Island Adventure Centre.
'The Buttress'

as well as developing a specialised technique. For the small cost involved, it would seem to be a very useful addition to any building where a climbing wall of the more traditional style already exists.

The frustration of fanatical climbers not infrequently finds relief in climbing on their own houses and many climbers have developed their own party pieces with which they confound their friends and amaze their neighbours. One such problem was a traverse of the former Chapel at *White Hall Open Country Pursuits Centre* at Buxton. While on the staff of the Centre, Joe Brown painstakingly worked out a complete traverse of the building and, through constant practice, was able to complete seven complete rounds wearing bedroom slippers and smoking a cigarette – few could do one traverse wearing the proper equipment (Plate 7).

A more sophisticated wall is available at *Drake's Island Adventure Centre* at Plymouth (Plate 8, Fig. 17). The wall, now known as 'The Buttress' was originally built to support anti-aircraft guns, the friable nature of the rock being unable to withstand the constant vibration from the guns. The Buttress was first used for climbing in 1960 and is now used as an introduction to climbing by some thirty young people every week. It is also used by some local youth clubs and schools. The climbs are about thirty feet

51

in length and vary in standard from *Difficult* to *Very Difficult*.[1] The construction of walls makes rope handling very simple and is ideal for demonstrations and practices for mountain rescue.

As a whole, the outdoor group of walls offer the closest approximation to natural rock climbing; they are often made inhospitable through wet and cold and frequently embody an element of objective danger from loose rock or recalcitrant authorities. They range from sophisticated structures costing over a thousand pounds to humble disused bridges and garden walls. It must be stressed, however, that even the most derelict looking building will be owned by someone, either privately or by a public authority and it is therefore essential to seek the permission of the owners before any climbing is undertaken.

All these walls suffer from the principle disadvantage that their use for beginners is so often limited by the vagaries of the British climate, a fact which strongly favours the use of the indoor type of wall which is now examined.

[1]The standards of climbs in Britain are graded as follows: easy, moderate, difficult, very difficult, severe, very severe, extremely severe.

4 Indoor Climbing Walls

There is a great variety of indoor walls; each type having its own particular advantages and disadvantages.

For the purpose of this book, they have been placed into the following categories: —

(1) Purpose built.
(2) Modifications to existing fabrics.
(3) Manufactured apparatus.

Undoubtedly there will be walls built in the future incorporating the better features of each of these categories.

(1) PURPOSE BUILT

The first purpose built wall in Britain was designed and erected by the Cumberland Education Authority and is a simple brick construction with the added refinements of concrete fins, wooden platforms and strips of wood and metal piping. It provides a good basis for learning the elementary skills but lacks variety in the type of holds available, and tends to develop a 'strong arm' approach to technique. Because of the verticality, large holds are required for beginners which later become unnecessary as skill develops. As there is no means of adjusting the wall except by 'elimination', the wall is limited in value for the more experienced climber.

Built in a similar fashion, the sheer size of the Liverpool wall has overcome the limitations of its type of construction as there is adequate space for all standards of climbs to be incorporated into the design.

A quite different approach to creating variety of climbs has been used at Scunthorpe where an ingenius method of varying the type and size of holds has been developed. The system used is the brain child of architect Lennard C. Anderson, who first used this method at the Royal Belfast Academy Institution. Routes of varying standard are readily created to match the abilities of the individual.

The most advanced development in indoor climbing walls is on the Wyndham Tower where natural stone has been used and rock climbing conditions have been simulated, which closely approach those on an actual rock face.

(1) Ullswater School, Penrith.
(2) Liverpool University.
(3) West Common Sports Hall, Scunthorpe.
(4) The Wyndham Tower, Cumberland.

Ullswater School, Penrith (Plate 9).

By 1960, the Cumberland Education Authority recognised the need for a rock climbing simulator and built a simple climbing apparatus into the end wall of the gymnasium at the Ullswater School, and so became the innovator of a facility which is becoming increasingly recognised as an essential element in school and community provision.

The wall which measures 18′ × 40′ is built with rustic engineering bricks, designed to withstand hard wear; joints have been raked out to provide finger and toe holds, and individual header bricks have been projected or recessed to provide hand and foot holds. A hardwood platform 9′ × 2′, grooved for finger and hand holds, is secured to the wall by five cantilever 'T' brackets built into the wall 7′ above floor level. A vertical reinforced concrete fin has been installed at right angles to the platform and parallel to the side wall to form a chimney 2′ 9″ wide by 7′ high. Three ring bolts have been set into the wall at ceiling height in positions suitable for belays or abseils and two pitons inserted for running belays on one exposed traverse. Two 1¼″ galvanised pipes have been set 2″ from the end wall above the platform at heights of 8′ and 11′ for overhang and hand traverse practice. A 3″ × 2″ hardwood ledge has been plugged into the two walls framing the corner 12″ above the floor and is used for stressing the importance of footwork and balance in traversing techniques. A basketball wall fixture has been strengthened and can be used as a belaying platform.

Later walls have included a 4″ × 2″ wood strip secured vertically 1″ from the wall to give lay-back practice and also a stone or brick buttress built up a height of 7′, providing a sloping slab angle for easier climbing.

The walls are used to teach children all the basic techniques; they learn also to have confidence in one another and develop a responsible attitude to the safety of others. They are introduced to ropes, karabiners, slings, etc., and become familiar with their use and, after a while, climb in a more relaxed and confident manner. The Physical Education Adviser for Cumberland recognises a climbing consciousness developing in the schools fortunate enough to possess a climbing corner. The main criticism of the Ullswater wall is its verticality, which necessitates large holds for the beginner, which later proved to be too large to motivate the experienced climber. Climbs with small holds would undoubtedly be attractive to the proficient climber.

The additional cost of constructing the wall suitable for climbing was £120, and the design took into account the need to avoid restricting the floor space and the safety of other users to the gymnasium. There are therefore no dangerous projections below 7′.

Liverpool University (Plate 10).

Built on the same principle as the Cumberland wall and using the indigenous qualities of the brick work, this wall has overcome to a degree the intrinsic limitations of this type of construction by the sheer space available for designing separate climbs of standards to suit all abilities.

The wall measures 30′ × 50′ and rises from a narrow balcony from 20′ above the sports hall floor giving an added feeling of exposure to an already exposed wall.

The various holds are formed by: protruding bricks, cavities, vertical cracks, recessed bricks, etc., with concrete ledges and fins set in the wall to provide belay stances, overhangs, mantelshelves and chimneys of varying widths.

The centre section of the wall is excellent for beginners and climbers of limited ability, whereas the climbs on the extreme right and left test the most expert and will probably defeat him at his first attempts to master them.

Ring bolts are set high on the wall to give points of attachment for protecting the climber on the wall. The detailed positions of the holds were designed on the drawing board and final 'tuning' was made as the wall was being completed. It should not be

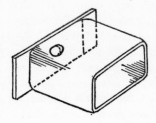

Fig. 18   Metal box built into a brick wall to accommodate various types of holds

thought that this type of wall, once constructed, cannot be adjusted; a competent bricklayer working under the direction of an experienced climber can modify the detailed holds on the wall. Indeed a small amount of replacement and pointing of the brick may occasionally be required.

The wall is used by the Department of Education in preparing students for visits to the Lake District Crags, and is also used by the University Climbing Club and other Colleges and Outdoor Organisations. The wall is undoubtedly successful, and is a well used facility.

As with many of the indoor walls, a criticism is the lack of easy angled climbing surfaces giving practice in slab climbing, and the wall would easily be improved by the inclusion of ring bolts for practising artificial tension climbing techniques.

The additional cost of constructing the wall over and above that of a normal end wall was approximately £600/£700.

West Common Sports Hall, Scunthorpe (Plate 11).

The wall was designed to provide inbuilt flexibility using a system of construction which facilitates a readily modified hold detail. Metal boxes are built into the wall, into which shaped wooden holds are inserted and secured by a bolt (Fig. 18). This method was devised by Leonard C. Anderson and used first in the climbing wall at the Belfast Academy Institution. The metal housings are placed at 2′ intervals vertically and 2′ 6″ horizontally. Into these housings are fitted beechwood blocks which can be recessed, fitted flush with the wall if no hold is required, or

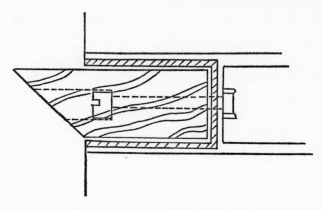

Fig. 19 The method of attachment of the beechwood
blocks in metal sockets

shaped and fitted to project from the wall. An unlimited variety of
shapes can be used, and there is remarkably little wearing or
damage to the holds which, in any case, can be easily and cheaply
replaced (Fig. 19 and Fig. 20).

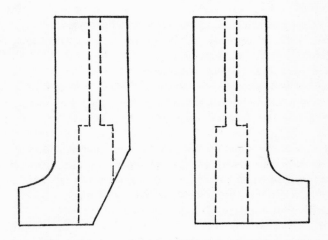

Fig. 20 Two styles of beechwood blocks

Vertical and horizontal cracks for fingers and toe holds have been provided for in the brick construction and there are ring bolts providing piton climbing.

At either end of the wall, a chimney climbing situation has been simulated by using the side walls in conjunction with a wood face supported by strutting; the whole construction has been covered by plywood. The almost frictionless surfaces provide difficult chimney climbing and one of the chimneys has been given a coating of cascamite and sand, thus providing a durable rough surface giving good frictional properties which reassures the beginner.

Small concrete ledges $3' \times 1\frac{1}{2}''$ provide overhang and mantel-self problems of a severity varied by the position from which they are attacked. The lower ledges provide practice at a psychologically secure level before an attempt is made to surmount the higher problem. The upper ledge also provides a belay and abseil stance.

An area of the wall has been tuned to meet the requirements of the beginner, whereas the more advanced climber and the expert also have their own areas on which to practice.

Initally protection was derived by threading the rope through the ring bolts at the top of the wall. This has now been superseded by a trackway which allows the rope to move across the wall, thus protecting the climb from directly above.

The difficult chimney has been extended upwards to give an additional six feet of climbing.

The wall has a symmetrical appearance which is aesthetically pleasing, and also has no projection below a height of 8' from the floor enabling team games, e.g. basketball and soccer, to be played without fear of injury due to the construction of the wall.

The wall has stimulated a great deal of interest and enthusiasm in an area not noted for the nurturing of the sport of rock climbing and those responsible for its provision are well satisfied that the additional cost of £900 has been well spent.

The Wyndham Tower (Fig. 21 and Plate 12)

The development of Climbing Walls by the Cumberland Education Authority has undoubtedly reached a high degree of sophistication at Wyndham Secondary School, and the 'Wyndham

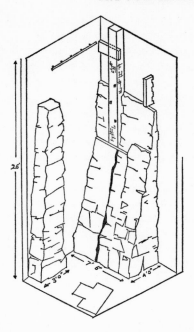

Fig. 21 The Wyndham Tower

Tower' probably simulates the natural situation more closely than any other artificial indoor structure.

In its original construction, it consisted of a tower 10 feet square by 25 feet high offering three climbing walls. The fourth wall of the tower, over the entrance, is made of fibreglass and allows daylight to pass through it.

Two of the climbing walls are constructed of rough-hewn St Bees sandstone blocks. These sandstone faces were built by a local stonemason; one being an inclined slope and the other being a near vertical pillar. The construction forms slabs, steep walls, cracks, chimneys, pillars, overhangs and mantelshelves; belaying points were also included. The third face and areas between the rock constructions are made of brick and protruding bricks which are used as hand and foot holds. The cost of the Tower in 1964 was £2,000; the estimated cost in 1968 is between

59

£3,000 and £3,500. In 1968, it was decided to add further features to the wall in order to broaden its scope, and two dedicated members of the school staff built an additional pillar. Building blocks were cemented and re-inforced with metal bars in the vertical holes of the blocks. The cost of materials for this additional 18′ buttress was £20.

As the Tower is a separate building, it is possible to restrict its use to experienced climbers and those under instruction. It is used for a total of 6 hours per week in school time and on three nights per week by Mountaineering Clubs and Youth Organisations.

The outstanding advantages of this type of wall are its use of natural stone, giving realism to the type and texture of the holds, its inclined surface gives practice in slab climbing and its isolation from other facilities makes the management and control of its use much easier. Classes of 20 can be readily catered for, and there are sufficient climbs to enable the improving climber to develop his skill.

2. Modifications to Existing Fabric

There are many examples of walls that have been produced by modifying the existing fabric or building, and a great deal can be achieved by the imaginative utilisation of existing fixtures.

1. Leeds University Department of Physical Education.
2. Meadow Boys' Club, Nottingham.

Leeds University Department of Physical Education (Plate 13)

In 1963, the Department of Physical Education was responsible for modifying an existing wall by removing sections of the brick work which was then either left as a cavity or infilled with a piece of natural rock carefully selected to give the size and shape of hold required for the practice of a specific technique (Plate 14). The wall is 62′ long and 15′ high, and includes three right angle corners in its length; two of these provide vertical arete climbs and the third approximates to the climber's 'corner'. A doorway provides the opportunity for chimney climbing techniques to be practised, i.e. back and foot and straddling.

Pitons have been placed in the wall to give protection and for the practice of abseiling and tension techniques and a small belay ledge has also been added.

17. Dring and Birtles wooden wall. *Ken Vickers*

18. Dring and Birtles wall adapted to simulate overhanging climbing. *Ken Vickers*

19. Ice Axe simulator. *S. Orr*

The tuning of the wall was accomplished with a fine sensitivity and great care was exercised in creating situations which could only be overcome by the techniques they were created to test. A good example of this is a vertical crack which is smoothed and shaped to provide no alternative other than an efficiently executed hand jam. This situation is further emphasised and the learning of the technique reinforced by the provision of poor sloping footholds which demand that the body is kept out from the wall, and a large proportion of the climber's weight is therefore taken by the hand-jams.

In general, the wall provides climbs of a high standard, and it was designed to test and extend the expert; in this it has most certainly succeeded.

Meadows Boys' Club

The Meadows Boys' Club, Nottingham, has, over the past decade, produced many enthusiastic and skilled young climbers who have made their mark in mountain explorations. Without any doubt, some of these young men were first motivated by the simple climbing wall created by modifying the brick work of the gymnasium housed in the Boys' Club building. As at Leeds, cavities have been made in the wall and then either left or filled in with natural stone. Pitons have been placed at strategic points and can be used for protection and for belays.

Metal structures supporting the roof have also been brought into use to provide climbing situations which simulate the climbing of a roof or overhang (Plate 15).

The modifications have cost nothing more than the labour involved and a few shillings for the additional pitons and yet the wall has provided the stimulus for many young men to learn the first principles of rock climbing, and provides a useful training area for the competent climber.

Modified in 1962, this wall is probably one of the earliest of its kind, and created a good deal of interest. Perhaps the success of the wall was assured by the participation, at the opening ceremony, of Don Whillans, one of Britain's foremost mountaineers. Apart from use by members of the Meadows Boys' Club, many other Youth Clubs, the Local Education Authority and some 40 scout units have used the wall for training over the last seven years.

E

It can be seen, in the case of the Leeds wall, that because of its limited height most of the interest will be in climbs which girdle the length of the wall a distance of 62'. Challenge can be artificially created by excluding holds above or below a particular course of bricks and by other methods of elimination. Competition can create an intense determination to overcome problems sometimes only inches above the ground, and in this situation the climber is able to concentrate solely on the technical difficulties without the added element of exposure. Where the problem is a difficult one, it may demand many attempts before the technique is perfected, and this will almost certainly provide incidental strength training which is a valuable feature of a vertical wall.

Once the problems of a route on the wall have been mastered and as skill develops, further elimination is necessary, or one can introduce the elements of repetition and speed; this is particularly advantageous if the object of the exercise is to develop strength and stamina. It is a simple matter to adapt the principles of interval training or progressive resistance training to a climbing wall.

3. MANUFACTURED APPARATUS
   (1) Hopkins Wall
   (2) Windsor Rock Climbing apparatus
   (3) Dring & Birtles, Leicester.

There are now a number of manufacturers producing apparatus which is sometimes described as portable climbing equipment. One of the earliest of these was the Hopkins Wall which was first built by a Physical Education Adviser for just over £16.

Hopkins Wall

Made of hardboard and built on a timber frame, the prototype was approximately 18' high by 4' 6" wide, and included such features as foot and hand holds, mantelshelves and holds for jamming and lay-backing. These holds were either cut into the hardboard or screwed to the surface and then covered with a mixture of cascamite and sand which closely resembles the texture of rock. The obvious advantage of this type of wall is its cheapness and its limited portability, which allows it to be erected indoors and out of doors and can be varied in angle to give variation in the difficulty of climbs. A number of such walls placed side by side would obviously increase the scope to include traversing, or would allow a number of parties to work at the same time. Hopkins, who is responsible for the wall's development, has made the point that it is possible to drill a group in the skills and disciplines of rock climbing and yet keep it interesting, even in the quiet of a suburban garden, so that each member of the group under instruction knows exactly what is expected of him before he attempts his big adventure in the mountains.

Windsor Rock Climbing Wall, Solihull

H. Hunt & Sons Ltd., gymnastic appliance manufacturers from Liverpool, have developed climbing equipment for inclusion in a school gymnasium known as the Windsor Rock Climbing Wall. The wall is illustrated and it can be seen that there are a large number of situations available for the practising of rock climbing techniques (Plate 16). The main feature of the adjustable wall is that it stores vertically flush with the building and can be pulled out, as a window ladder, to form a chimney situation in conjunction with a gymnasium wall or can be climbed at angles variable from a slab to overhang. The surface of the wall is covered with holes so that it resembles a large peg board into which individual hand and foot holds are plugged. A tension climb can be practised by plugging small ring bolts into the peg board in the same way that hand and foot holds are put in. There are attachments at the top of the wall to give protection to those practising abseiling and wooden strips placed on the wall are arranged to give practice in traversing. At the corner of the walls, a platform has been fixed to enable practice in belaying and pitch climbing to be simulated.

A further development has been to modify the brickwork of the gymnasium wall by projecting a large number of bricks which are numbered; climbs can then be devised using different combinations of holds. One might start with a beginners group by asking them to simply climb the wall using as many holds as they wish; progress can be made by limiting the holds to odd numbered holds only and so the process can be continued giving climbs of increasing difficulty. Similarly, the peg board frame can provide good fun by a game of follow my leader, where the leader of the group reduces the number of holds by removing them until the absolute minimum is reached.

Because of the limited height of the wall, many activities can be engaged in without the use of top ropes and this can, with little stimulation from the teacher, provide a most enjoyable and vigorous activity in addition to its initial purpose of teaching rock climbing skills and rope handling drills.

Dring & Birtles Indoor Rock Climbing Apparatus (Plates 17 and 18).

Dring & Birtles have developed a method of reproducing rock climbing situations similar to the system devised by the French in the early 1950s. The advantage of this particular type of construction is that it can be used to clad the interior of any type of building and is therefore suitable for installing in any situation.

The wall is built in units or modules and a basic wall may be added to and a more sophisticated apparatus built up. A variety of climbs can be devised as the apparatus makes use of the peg board system of modifying holds and an interesting development is the overhang simulator (Plate 18) which very closely approaches a natural situation as pitons may be inserted at varying distances.

5 Artificial Devices

The diversity of climbing walls reflects the ingenuity of the climbers who have been largely responsible for their development and it is no surprise that they have turned their inventiveness to the construction of specialised equipment designed to test techniques which cannot be incorporated on a standard wall.

THE FALLING CLIMBER SIMULATOR (Fig. 22)

At Plas y Brenin, the National Mountaineering Centre, it has been found worthwhile, in introducing beginners to rock climbing, to give them some idea of the weight of a second or leader coming on to the rope. There are many simple devices which have been used to simulate this situation and the guillotine devised at Plas y Brenin is possibly the most sophisticated so far constructed.

It consists of two 30′ parallel scaffold tubes braced and welded top and bottom. It stands vertically in a concrete block and is bracketed on to the wall at the top, standing clear some 2′ or so. Moving freely, vertically, is a metal slide to which is bolted a concrete block giving a total weight of ten stones. With the aid of a windlass and wire rope, the weight can be raised to any height desired, and with a release hook operated from below with a cord the block is triggered. For safety reasons, three car tyres are embedded in the concrete block as a shock absorber. The person arresting the block stands on a convenient platform half way up alongside the upright tubes and is firmly belayed to points above and below using pitons cemented into the wall. Well padded at waist and wearing gloves and helmet, the pupil takes in as the block is raised and brakes and arrests it as it falls. This is done from progressively greater heights until it starts above and passes the pupil. With a running belay fitted on top of the frame, it will be seen that an upward pull can be imparted.

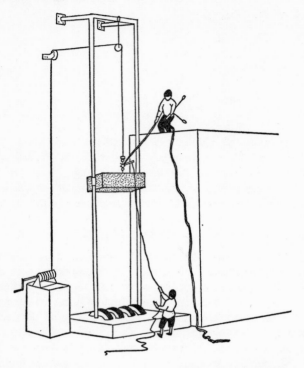

Fig. 22 A falling climber simulator. Plas y Brenin, North Wales

A short period using this device is programmed for all pupils prior to climbing on major crags in the district. The difference and effectiveness of shoulder or waist belay can easily be discovered and the pupil quickly gains confidence before embarking on a climb.

THE ICE-AXE BRAKING SIMULATOR
Sometimes known as Crauford's Contraption (Plate 19)

This device was used at the Bellahouston Mountain Safety Exhibition and consists of a sloping board approximately 40′ by 7′ with an upturned run out at the bottom. Steps were placed at one side of the board in order to reach the point from which one slides down the slope. The ice pick is placed into a narrow channel. Underneath this slot is a heavy wood runner onto which is mounted a rubber brake pad.

Provided that the correct pressure is placed on the runner, via the ice-axe, the braking pad is pressed firmly to another pad and the climber is brought to a stop in a controlled manner. If, however, the ice-axe is used incorrectly, it is not unusual for it to be wrenched from the climber's hand when the stopper is reached, whilst the climber continues down the slope and is arrested by the run out. It is necessary to keep the board at a steep angle to get maximum effect, i.e. 1 in 5 to 10 and to have it fixed rigidly.

6 Conclusions

Whereas it is difficult to provide a concise summary of climbing walls based on such a mass of differing factual information, it is both possible and desirable to stress the most important factors which should influence planners and designers. These should be:

(1) adaptability
(2) durability
(3) safety
(4) cost

ADAPTABILITY

Walls should provide a full range of climbing which will not only encourage the novice but will equally stimulate the expert. Several of the walls discussed have attempted to solve this problem.

DURABILITY

This factors depends largely on the extent of use and on the materials of construction. Most walls have not been in existence long enough to make a valid assessment of their durability but there is already evidence to suggest that the life of any climbing wall will be prolonged by the use of P.A.s or gym shoes.

SAFETY

On an artificial wall, the element of controlled danger is much less a part of the incentive than in the case of real climbing. Because most walls are readily available to novices, authorities responsible for running such walls have an undeniable responsibility for making adequate safety arrangements. This can only be achieved either by denying access to the wall except under expert supervision, or by making only the lowest section of the wall accessbile to novices. Whatever provisions are made, it is essential that adequate safety regulations are prominently displayed. These rules will necessarily vary from wall to wall, but advice ought to be sought in their writing from the Regional Committees of either the British Mountaineering Council or the Central Council of Physical Recreation.

COST

The cost of a wall depends largely on its size and its degree of sophistication; it is generally true to say that these factors are directly proportional to cost. The potential demand should therefore be established in order to provide the most suitable wall.

These four factors can rightly be regarded as the most important and provided that they are sensibly interpreted the future of climbing walls is assured.